Techne's Clearinghouse

Techne's Clearinghouse

John Foy

Zoo Press

Zoo Press • P.O. Box 3528 • Omaha, Nebraska 68103
Printed in the United States of America

Distributed to the trade by The University of Nebraska Press
Lincoln, Nebraska 68588 • www.nebraskapress.unl.edu

Cover design by Janice Clark of Good Studio © 2004
www.goodstudio.com

Library of Congress Cataloging-in-Publication Data

Foy, John, 1960-
  Techne's clearinghouse / John Foy.
    p. cm.
  ISBN 1-932023-20-8 (pbk. : alk. paper)
  I. Title.

PS3606.O959T43 2004
811'.6--dc22

                                    2004020345

zoo29

First Edition

Acknowledgments

I would like to thank the editors of the following publications, in which some of the poems in this manuscript first appeared:

The Antigonish Review: "The Orangutan" (from "Le Jardin des Plantes") and sections from the "Rue des Martyrs" sequence; *Columbia:* "Party On The Boat"; *Graham House Review:* "Lauterbrunnen," "The Watusi," "The Cape Vulture," "The Panther" (from "Le Jardin des Plantes") and sections from the "Rue des Martyrs" sequence; *The Lyric:* sections from the "Rue des Martyrs" sequence; *The New Criterion:* "The Disappearance of Saint-Exupéry" and sections from the "Rue des Martyrs" sequence; *The New Yorker:* "Local Superstition"; *Parnassus: Poetry in Review:* "Eucalyptus Trees," "A Minority of One," "At Shinglekill Creek" and "Voyager 2, An Elegy" (from "Lacrimae Rerum"); *Poetry:* sections from the "Rue des Martyrs" sequence; *Southwest Review:* "Pledges of Secrecy" and "Subterranean Cities."

"Pledges of Secrecy," originally published in *Southwest Review*, appeared on the *Poetry Daily* Web site. "Commander" and "Paterfamilias" originally appeared on the *BigCityLit* Web site. "The Shearwater" originally appeared on the *Flâneur* Web site.

to my mother
and the memory of my father

Table of Contents

But thou didst love the world.

—Marlowe

I. Things in Heaven and Earth

Eucalyptus Trees

(Brejal, state of Rio de Janeiro)

Look how their longing has mastered them.
      Purged of every impulse
            but the will to rise,

each a chancellor now,
         they tower single-mindedly
            out along the road.

No doubting their affinity
         with whatever strives to disengage itself
            from all those baser elements:

the riotous bamboo, the dutiful hedge,
         the coy azalea bush that casts
            aspersions in the dirt.

These, the eucalyptus trees,
         avail themselves of the empyreal,
            high tops tossed at altitudes

where only wind prevails
         —how pale and tenuous
            their visible commitment to the earth.

No wonder, then, they leave behind
         the rougher skin, as contemplatives
            let fall away the trappings of this world,

consigning to oblivion
         the shirts they'll never use again.
            Stripped thus, the eucalyptus trees ascend,

saudade their abstract attribute,
    a yearning for the spires
        they wish they could become.

It's a predilection for air and light
    that keeps them reaching
        after higher signatures,

a time unheard of here,
    in a key the wind, poor hint,
        can only do its best to emulate.

And yet these trees,
    despite the lift and loft,
        still hear some note of the tellurian:

every eucalyptus leaf hangs down,
    pointing backward, lured by gravity,
        dependent on a lower origin.

This delicate contrariety,
    an interplay of bearings
        the mind at once

can apprehend before it understands,
    gives each tree its philosophic look,
        as though the foliage were pondering,

like Seneca, the state of things,
    the dark ancestral root
        holding tree and truth

firmly to the subterranean,
    and a million eucalyptus leaves
        called to another life, kindled

to rise again as perfume now
    in the hills all around,
        the smoke of eucalyptus

homesick for the supernatural
    and good, too, for keeping flies away,
        a method much used in these parts.

The Angel Catcher

*(after a sculpture by Marcelyn Gow
based on drawings by John Hejduk)*

How terrible that the gleaming device
should have already taken shape,
not merely in the loft of the mind, as conception,
but as object, here, in the empire of clocks,
knives, and particle accelerators.
I have seen the Angel Catcher.
Stainless steel, glinting chromium blue,
almost criminal, it hangs on what's human
like a backpack frame, held in place
by rudimentary belt and shoulder straps.
Atop the frame, in fan formation,
eight long hollow-point spikes.
A contraption, elegant in design,
for fixing things in heaven and earth
that go undreamt of in our philosophy.
The metal spikes afflict the angels,
who, pierced or impaled, collapse into physics,
entering the world as meteorites
plummeting toward the South China Sea.
How strange that this corporeal instrument
should presuppose that which drifts beyond
the limit of gauge and control. What animosity!
Will we capture angels with this thing,
bring them in as prisoners,
or merely torment the flying enemy?
Of course, angels never *really* catch on a pike's point
like vulgar plastic bags. They are, though,
susceptible to implication,
driven off, wounded, killed by the spike's threat,
its malign intention ravaging their higher sphere.
How sad, this testament to angels, a pointed gesture
indicating the end of inquiry.

Local Superstition

O my old night house.
I walk your property again
under five white stars
to see my rusted fence, my rock,
my maple tree—still there,
still chillingly legitimate.
Deer in the dark
move along the wood line
like the ghosts of débutantes
who've died violently and don't remember.

In my pocket your keys
on the galvanized ring,
hard old shiners
dying to be used.
I'm tired of their obsessive pleading.
I won't go through your doors,
afraid as I am of the dogs,
the basement. She's in there,
accusatory, sad,
sitting with her 12-gauge shotgun
and her big tin pots.

What about the analyst,
that expensive friend
who'd intercede for a fee?
What will he do with his candle,
stuck on the first step
down into your storm cellar,
a Grendel waiting for him,
prehistorically hungry?

No need to summon the professionals.
No remuneration
for hankering around the night house.
I crouch judiciously behind my rock
reciting weird Norwegian names
to drive off the doppelgänger.

Will her voice come back tonight
to this periphery?
I used to swear I'd follow her
to caves in the Carpathian Mountains,
that I'd bear up
under the rain-heavy docks of the world
like a human cantilever.
But even this last vow
has fetched up on nails.

Ouro Prêto

(for Roberto and Maria-José Lanari)

1

The children have no bicycle,
and if they have a dog, it's a worried,
inquisitive amalgam of dust,
but they do have kites:
homemade bamboo crosses
webbed with cheap translucent paper
—green, orange, red, blue,
utterly perishable.
Not long after dawn,
as though they'd come up with the sun,
fifty of them wiggle in the sky
over Antonio Dias
and the School of Mines
and the hovels on the hill.

2

The woman at the pension kitchen
where we eat lunch is eighty-one, at least.
She comes from the opposite side of town
on foot, gradually, without a stick.
Her legs, little more than canes,
are tough, unulcered, soldierly.
Up the rua Sacramento
she moves like an image pulled along
in the Procession of the Dead *Senhor*.
Her face, a clawed triangle hewn backwards,
mouth cut neatly in the front,
is impotent and durable
as the cooked chicken's foot
she chews on patiently for lunch.

3

In the library at night,
lost in Volume III
of *Milling Methods in the Americas*,
I read about molybdenite recovery
and the metallurgy of zirconium.
None of it brings me closer
to *Itacolomy*, "old stone boy"
out there in the dark,
a peculiar rock formation
on the south horizon.

Outside in the steep,
cobbled street, looking up,
I see the Southern Cross,
comeliest of constellations
vying with Centaurus
in the pageant of the sky.

From the stone bridge
bracing the ravine, I see
the red roofs, dark now, the color of beans,
and the Church of Santa Efigênia,
pretty as illuminated pyrite
in her floodlit robe.
Lanterns among the stacked *favelas*
wink and shine
like spirits in the hills
throwing a party
for the moon over Ouro Prêto.

Later, as I lie in bed
listening to pigeons on the roof,
St. John of *Revelation* comes to mind.
No geophysicist, but still he knew the names
of the parti-colored stones of paradise:
chrysolite, beryl, amethyst.

4

I sat all morning on the old stone wall
above Antonio Dias,
mackerel rooftops, dirty backyards,
banana trees in the ravine.

That hemorrhaging Christ
is depicted here in every church.
Had he ever come to Ouro Prêto
to wash himself off in the circular fountain
at the ringing of the bells?
Maybe he led a pack mule up the hill
to Cachoeira das Andorinhas
(where the creek meets the precipice)
or went down the cobbled street
in dirty plastic thongs.

Did he love the *candeia* smoke,
the cry of goats,
the sunlight in bright doorways?
No one here believes
he would forsake the Brazilian highlands.

His face, everywhere in Ouro Prêto
(you'd think he'd been born here),
is made to tell not only of time
like the walls of Antonio Dias,
but of all the accumulated sorrow,
and the eyes, unassuming
as the kites of the poor,
look out with clarity
into the terror of things to come.

He would have known these housetops,
the pigeons,
the laundry in the wind.

Burnt Hill

(Morro da Queimada, Ouro Prêto)

Nothing up there in the fog
can lay more claim to permanence than chickens
tilling in the ditch or the peripatetic dog
not committed to much, thin as a wrench,
digesting destiny beneath a truck
equipped with blocks and patron saint.

Everyone has a patron saint:
good-for-nothings in the fog,
donkeys, drivers of trucks,
even the Morpho butterfly, and chickens,
and those performing wonders with a wrench.
The saints are only visible to dogs.

Given to worm and tick, the dogs
come and go, perplexed, and saints
try to grip wrenches
with unrealistic hands of fog.
The meal of choice, for dogs: whatever chicken
gets dispatched by Gilson's truck.

Only the chosen own a truck
—even they go nowhere. Some have a private dog
or a few embittered chickens
running in circles. Only days and saints
are plentiful, and mountain fog,
and boys who clang old buckets with a wrench.

Much can be done with mattock, jack, and wrench,
especially if one owns a truck
and gets up early in the fog,
by 5:00 A.M., before the dogs
can chase away the apparitional saints.
Things always need delivering, like chickens.

They get served up in their own chicken
blood, and men as practical as Locke use wrenches
to justify their homes or nail a saint
above a bed or fix the fender of a truck.
The dogs, not schooled like Pavlov's dog,
live in perpetual fog.

The saints do what they can for truck
and chicken, jack and wrench,
and dogs footing through the fog.

Ismene

. . . that beauteous measure of the ordinary.
—Kierkegaard

Where did you go, Ismene,
with your cowl and canvas bag?
Toward which hill did you set out
in your thin, unsuitable slippers
when the smoke and blood had settled
down into the dust of Thebes?
By then in shock
and finally beyond the laws
decreed by a deluded king,
you dug a hole for your Antigone.

How you met death went utterly ignored.
You walked away, just walked away
from the hobnailed bludgeon of the gods
to perish in the hills,
dying beneath the Pleiades
one night, unmangled.
Now you are with Elpinor
—altogether gone, a band
trekking across the quiet basins
of the underworld.

Back in the bright,
those who fight with pointed instruments
give no thought
to insubstantial girls in hell.
But one, who fears obscurity,
has taken time to think of you
shivering at the perimeter,
the queen of oblivion now,
an unquestionable
nobody, even down among the dead.

A Minority of One

Dracula can't help himself,
still tethered by hunger to an earth
where all his appetites are criminal
—his mere existence
an offense punishable by death.
Who can understand the toll
the nightshift takes
on this aristocrat? Alone
he must attend his bats
and the beautiful, albeit dead,
whey-faced girls, once nubile victims,
now part of the entourage.
They get to stay in the Transylvanian Alps
caning the wolves. Dracula,
meanwhile, abroad in London,
whiffling around at night,
perching on gables in the wind,
standing in dark corners
trying to survive.
Then there's Renfield,
useless really but the only friend,
grubbing in the dirt for centipedes.
Isn't that the way it always is?
Even Dracula panics
among the locked minds unable
to believe in ghosts
and wary of longevity.
Dracula the immigrant
with not even one full-witted friend
in the realm of probability,
and nowhere a willowy teenage virgin
unsure of her own mind
—each one gainfully employed
or in the hands of therapists.

The Disappearance of Saint-Exupéry

Beyond the airfield, near Chelles,
a farm and poplars gesture in the heat.
You dream, in your way, of Senegal,
and we sit by the hangar, all too aware
of the indignities of flightlessness.
We watch the bright planes
coming in, heading off,
as though this were all a game.
The day drones, and the wind picks up
as it did for that final mission
of Saint-Exupéry, a man versed
in aerial contingencies.
What a clean departure from the earth,
to disappear silently from tracking systems.
A routine flight from Corsica,
the airstrip at evening, the first lights,
his leather jacket open, hanging down.
Then the night, the Mediterranean,
the pilot in his craft, rising.

Refugium

If what Diotima said was true,
then Love's the only child of Poverty,
a mendicant, that's all, with neither shoes
nor bed, and yet adept at wizardry
and rites of every kind, with messages
for those like us, under Gemini,
walking down by where the demiurge
dwells among things that don't abide;

and who's to say Love isn't with us now,
commending my old shoes, your lived-in shirt,
our aspiration in the lost art
of casting spells, revealing here below
that a little divination, born of dirt,
can bring together all the broken parts.

Late Summer Idylls

1. The Barn

Here we are again, the summertime
like one big pavilion,
and you and I among the birds.
You're reading Gombrich now, on the Ideal,
bikini top unstrung and dropped away
to let those thoroughbreds respire.
How they've pressed themselves upon the mind,
calling to be touched and thought about
and taken in the hands.
The breeze of Praxiteles' ghost
comes here to concur. He cannot rest
with so much loveliness to gander at
and still so many who would disavow
dear Eros, that old-time friend.

2. The Storm

We've had a little respite,
it hasn't been
half long enough, from the city's
vast accumulation
of petty annoyances.
Why do we live the way we do,
chasing what turns out to be
no more than some rusty pail?
Though I too participate in
the delusions of the world,
I sit out on the stoop right now
as August thunder, still far off,
turns over in its mind
what is to become of us.

3. The Spring Behind Pat's House

I'd like my words to come
unbeckoned and continuously,
the way the water under us
runs over the impediment of stone,
moving with such eloquence,
in an idiom so free of doubt,
that I begin to see
how wrong I've been, neglecting everywhere
nature's quiet disquisition
—the water just goes on and on,
obeying gravity the way I'd want
my own words to be inclined,
speaking irrefutably
from the bed of logic and desire.

At Shinglekill Creek

(for Catherine, my daughter)

Like water, here, in a standing wave,
the marriage of a forward-surging force
and some impediment (a limestone laved
for years and years, down in and up against
what it can and cannot modify),
a brief inflection only, in the sphere
of all that might be said when water rides
the wave it makes, its involution there
under the backwash, white, a falling back
upon itself, the water in the trough
still craving the endearments of a curve,
the up-and-over held against a rock
on which a voice quickens that cannot have,
but *does*, no rule or sense of what's enough.

Commander

(for Christopher, my son, at 15 months)

Stones and water, water, stones
—a brute piece of planet
you can hold in your hand
and the splash you can bring about
at will, a clean hit
upon the cool and Heraclitean.

You fix a blue, absolving eye
on these elements that figure
pleasurably in the mind.
They've come to occupy your time,
as much as we can give you here
by a cognac-colored brook that goes along
beneath a wooden plank
quietly, as it has for years
no one has seen fit to count,
its current here and now
shivered by the stones
you throw down purposefully,
like some commander high atop
the promontory of Chimerium.

Could it be that you would never stop,
if the pile of stones I put
by your right hand were always there,
and the light this April afternoon
were not bound to fail,
and my patience were without end?
You, my hoplite, throwing stones
at the brook for another thousand years.
It's only right, only fair
that we leave you for a time
to your stones and water,
your water and your stones.

To Have and To Hold

(for my daughter, at 10 months)

You hold it up, Catherine, to give to me,
this warm Brazilian dirt, a quantity

of dust in your hand that slips away.
You're learning still to get the gravid weight

and feel of things in a here and now
that constitute just what the world allows

and in whose tutelage you've proudly found
the face of the earth, as though *its* ground

were your own, and this the only hill
endowed with summer's long, maternal,

infiltrating light, and you by decree
the queen of it all. You offer me

some more, the goodly dirt, oblivious
to what you really do and don't possess.

How, on earth, could it be otherwise?
The mind at first must wait upon the eyes,

functioning as pure sensorium
without pretending yet to hold its own

in the almost unthinkable abstract.
Apprenticed lovingly to objects,

it thereby fits itself for later flight
away from them, out toward what might

or might not be, the grand conceptual.
It's too soon, though, to spurn the visible,

the oldest of our friends, whose common dust
employs the mind, inclining us to trust

this dirt the saints are ready to invoke
as wage in the emporiums of smoke.

Enough! I shall protect you for a time,
but how can I claim to own you, Catherine,

when I can't even claim to own these words,
which only lend themselves from a hoard

of which I, too, partake, till I'm the one
possessed, my measure due at last to them.

You'll soon be vested here and pay the price
for holding things abstractly. I've paid twice:

laboring for some perfect point of view
and dreaming always of exactitude.

You're getting the idea, though, the touch
of elemental ownership, clutching

matter briefly in your small hand.
In this way you'll begin to apprehend

the paucity of substance here, the dust
and dirt, the earth dying as it does

in a world mostly given to accidence
and fancy lights—whose utter loveliness

I, your father, cannot disavow.
My father, whom you barely knew, is now

maintained as ashes in a box,
unprepossessing and without a lock,

that holds the shriven substance he's become.
In this form, he would have me think again

about Bellagio and World War II,
the steady breeze off Brighton Pier, and you

my little bird, with your box of shapes,
the prize possession of your small estate.

I give you what I have. The fireflies
tonight, like luminescent promises

happening all around us on the path,
regardless of whatever comes to pass,

will hold you rapt and wed you to a world
where, in time, to have is to be had.

II. Rue des Martyrs

Rue des Martyrs

(for Majô)

1

All I've really wanted is to catch
the birds of my cold-water garret
seven flights above rue des Martyrs.
King of sirens, bells, and wind,
Orion's Belt beyond my railing,
I've watched the moon rise
like a white pigeon, by far
the fairest ever to appear
but given now in perpetuity
to the nighttime sky.
I've tried to build what nests I could
in whatever cracks I could find
or make in the world's bird-killing
black granite face.

2

In that cold first hour
before even the butcher's wife is out of bed,
we sit in the dark, looking out
into dismals of winter fog
that have clung about the habitations
of this city for some two thousand years.
The bulb in our refrigerated room
is the first light in the channel to shine.
I know most would call it a sick habit,
this raw, too-early
waking to the dead December buildings.
But there is comfort in our vigil,
a wild relief in looking out
at starlings on the chimney pots.

3

I have a sense of place
in this room enriched by scarcity:
unadorned walls, cold-water sink,
our cracked casement window
where I hear the bells that ring
—the sound of things required
among the domes of Sacré-Coeur,
unconditional domes, in mist, rising
like something hardly real,
a vision that may or may not exist,
though that distinction is ineligible
up here among hoodlum pigeons
at the quiet drifting edge,
where I've come to find a place of sense.

4

I'm sure he was, in the strict,
clinical sense, an idiot.
I sat at my café as he trundled by
like an eight-sided wheel:
no shrapnel of intelligence
in the craters he had for eyes,
his legs contending with his hips,
a loosened lower lip,
his gibbon arms in the air
with a mind of their own.
He gripped a loaf of bread and a pear,
poor man, some mother's tragedy
in the perfectible world,
his necktie knotted perfectly.

5

At work the supervisor summoned me,
asking with an MBA's tone control
and six-mile concern if I were really
going about life in responsible
fashion, providing for the future,
attempting to maximize my options
with the company, and did I nurture
outside interests, perhaps have some fun
with hobbies? Was I happy? Did I
still live in the attic? The years ahead?
What could I, in their employ, do but lie.
Would they have understood if I had said,
like Nietzsche's inquirer, that I'd seen
poor logic curl about itself and scream?

6

I wouldn't mind going crazy.
Not deeply, irrevocably mad
—just a little, enough to reach release,
to be put in hospital for a while.
I wouldn't mind the nurses when they'd come
with warm fluids, I wouldn't mind, at night,
the orderlies in the green corridor.
I'd welcome the hours of reflection,
the time I could use to muse upon
the alarmingly infinite network
of relations and their analogies.
I'd welcome whatever came,
encourage the shy appearance
of the triangle and the clear blue sphere.

7

Did you hear something in the corridor,
a complaint on the landing,
the rattle of a long-neglected door
touched by night drafts in the building?
Did Madame Antonini climb the stairs?
Would she be in the storage room
at 3:00 A.M., bedeviled and sere,
looking for spiders to kill with a spoon?
Didn't you hear it? I heard something
like wind in the wires, a knock,
someone somewhere crying
more softly than my bitter clock,
something barely audible
transpiring at the bottom of the hall.

8

Coming from the bathroom at 4:00 A.M.,
hesitating by the stairs
in civilization's attic,
light bulbs blown out long ago,
I'm braced to see what I pray I won't,
some unholy wailing raw-head
spinning itself out
from the most inhospitable part of the self
to dog the other parts to death.
Or would I see a species of angel,
something out of Botticelli
gazing preternaturally
as a mother would upon her child,
who finds you here, just where she thought you'd be?

9

The question isn't whether I see ghosts
but whether they see me,
relatives arriving blindly
from the reverse side of fact,
a bewildering trip.
They signal not the end of sanity
but the sharpening of the eye,
sanity only a clinical gauge
of the extent to which vision is impaired.
We speak fearfully, like tourists,
of "the dark place" and "the dunes of the dead,"
when we ought to speak of home,
whose terminals, alive, we are,
the ghosts coming to relieve our loneliness.

10

I know that animals too can dream
in the heat, behind machines
where I am thinking about the activity of the brain
as an Asian hunger would listen in a cage at night
except that yesterday we watched the gibbons
with a deep sense of vocation,
a fond feeling, almost nostalgia,
that could not get beyond the primordial wham
as though the distribution of star systems
particles and waves
changing their personalities
might teach us how to go calmly
up the tubular horns of oblivion
to the far side of my bitter will to pray.

11

In holey socks and underpants
I lay on the garret floor,
closed my eyes, perspired, waited,
listening to Gregorian chants,
one high, lonely, incorporeal tenor
crystalline even on my cheap tape deck,
the rattling little piece of Sony plastic
that I used but hated.
I tried, like St. Anthony,
to ignore the cracked, plaster window frame
and the floorboards under me, refractory
and warped in that galling game,
the cenobite inside his cell
clawed by the terrestrial.

12

Whatever I hungered for I got,
since every piece of slaughtered thing was there,
disjointed in the stalls of the market
not far from the bottom of my stairs.
The cushy, pastel-colored tongues of cows,
glabrous kidneys, rinsed and ready brains,
brownish blood-packed pigs' bowels,
tooled rabbits dangled upside-down, blood drained
into the plastic headbags, a chicken
hooked with a hook through its withered anus,
fish unzipped and dying in the bins,
a toothy goat head, lips against the glass.
No blade to jugular, no fire prayer.
All I had to do was go downstairs.

13

Who are you, there, in the rain,
in a doorway, at a corner, on the steps
of a large municipal building?
Who are you, with only overcoat,
without domicile, in the public way?
You are, *mon ami*, an outdoor man,
an indictment of what I am
and what little I can claim to own,
my poor tenacities.
Everything was wrecked and wrong (I thought so!
Your discrimination was an outrage!)
when in my pity and guilt
I offered you coins and a Métro pass,
you declined, I put them in your coat.

14

I stopped awhile to watch the girls
doing what they do
under favorable lights
along Boulevard Rochechouart,
where naked, bending adolescents held the eye.
Men came here alone to try
the calculated mouth of promise,
the trade the street is given to.
Behind the lacing of the neon lights,
the buildings' edges zippered up the night,
and there was nothing new except the faces
of young bodies, pliable and used,
held in the old dance
under a poker-faced moon.

15

When I return one day to where I'm from,
I will, I know, revert
to the cataleptic language of home
if I hope to communicate
with those who chose to stay behind.
I went away with Numidian cranes
to the abandoned rim of words,
a preserve I could barely say
in the language of home, where they grew old.
I no longer believe it's true
that people deteriorate from age;
it's only what they say to be consoled.
Maybe they grow unused to languages
that for a world of reasons they no longer use.

16

My railing shimmers. Ninety-five degrees,
a dead blue sky, the window open wide,
not a bird in the air, no shade, no breeze.
I keep quiet, lie on the sheets, don't try
to wage a war against necessity
in the barbaric afternoon heat.
I hide in the language of Sophocles
by the cool crossroad where three paths meet.
I bathe in the waters of a high rock spring
at the sanctuary, austere and steep,
penetrating twenty-four centuries.
I pray to the Eumenides that sing,
whose voices clear a pathway to the deep,
and I walk awhile beside Antigone.

17

Why she lived across the street
I cannot say. She'd set up shop
in the hackneyed suburbs
and told me once that she was an anarchist,
using the word too loosely
for the dermatologist she was,
packaged in one of the clean lifestyles.
"If not that," she said, trying to be clear,
"I'm at least a marginal.
I don't care for politicians."
She hated the way
elections were won, how freely
destinies were hung up
in the evanescence of a smile.

18

During a winter windstorm
the skylight window in the hallway
got blown back and broke.
The glass pane is a thing of the past.
The building's owner hasn't fixed it yet,
and the concierge doesn't give a damn
—our attic condition doesn't count.
So the elements come closer now.
I can look right up into storm or stars
from the corridor at night.
Often this March, when the moon is out,
a vertical shaft of blue light
stands there in the hallway
like a woman I used to know.

19

I look out from my weather-cracked window
at lights on the horizon at night
—a thousand propositions. Three compel the eye:
a red, blue, and green all in a line
between the Panthéon and St. Sulpice.
Luminaries keeping their distance,
three weird lithium girls
beyond time's power to dispel,
their desire safely disembodied
which otherwise could move the world.
Each night they come back glimmering
with Aristotelian clarity
—no question yet, no overture,
but already they know my name.

20

Sick of decision,
trying to fix with pins a way to know,
I look across at the cheap curtains
drawn for evening in that window
like mine, where the Portuguese couple
live with their black-and-white two-bit bird
chittering blindly on the decayed sill.
I smell their cooking. In the courtyard
fried rice and onions decorate the air,
and the impecunious moon comes up clean
to nickel-plate the buildings. Out there
like alien coins my decisions gleam,
just small change in time,
minted by will, not worth a *centime*.

21

She comes to me
when I am in the middle of the most desperate acts
in the barbed-wire yard of depravity.
She touches me
when I am involved in the shredded metal
of derailments and explosions,
when I am drugged and fixed underneath
the play of surgical instruments
in operations for which I have no coverage,
when I am lost among gasoline fires
and sweating at the slack orifice of the world.
She comes to me
with firsthand reports, in fabulous languages,
that say I'm still alive.

III. The Tears of Things

Pledges of Secrecy

I

How could he have known what he would find?
Heavy fighting continued in the mountains,
a lawless place, for many the last,
where automatic weapon exchanges
broke up evenings in the Central Range.
All the plans that had been made
came to have no application there.
He conceived the idea that his few belongings,
fueled by an implacable hatred
of their servitude and brutishness,
had formed a constituent assembly
against him—another hindrance.
He inferred that there were no instructions,
there had never been *any* instructions.

II

I won't discourage you from coming here
if that's what you truly want to do.
But then I'd hate for you to be deceived,
coming to this extremity
with cheap, therapeutic confidence
and an unrealistic expectation
of the rewards within this range,
deployed like antipersonnel mines
beneath the fluctuating surfaces
of the future—not just your own,
though disappointment might make you think this
for a while, but the future of the enterprise.
Should you decide to come, bring a rifle,
and don't let my condition frighten you.

Orpheus—World Tour

Down into the stadium
he came and sang for us,
three hundred thousand packed
in darkness cut by scything lights,
the old power of his song
fraught now with rage,
the no-longer-subtle grieving
engineered and amplified.

The voice of Orpheus crashed over us,
the militant longing wired
and towering from the black cliff,
such bitter majesty
that girders and floodlights wept.
Radio towers bowed their heads.
A Doric column of light
rose from the vent of our desire,
and the Taenarian Gate,
portal to the underworld,
rattled on its massive hinge.

In unity with him
we raged at our condition,
though stamp and clap was all we could do,
all that was left us,
legions of shades
lost and unrecognizable.
Orpheus, older than hell, come all this way,
and we with no news of his bride.

Subterranean Cities

They rented rooms in a low house by tracks
in the industrial area,
where freighters from Greece and Liberia
lay together under cranes, and the stacks
of so many chthonian factories
blew out into the sky the stink and boom
of manufacturing inside rooms
as big as subterranean cities.
Not far beyond the backyard of their home
the blue refinery fires burned,
and men went back and forth in trucks to earn
a kind of living in the outer zone.
They stayed out there among the chemical tanks,
thinking of cadmium and other things.

Sunken Waste Containers

Each night now I dream
about the things you've thrown away,
the sunken waste containers
at the bottom of the East River.

They loom together
in the mercury-contaminated muck,
ugly bolted modules
meant to be put out of mind.

Whatever doesn't fit or work
or can't be utilized immediately
or tranquilized
gets neatly jettisoned.

How could you function otherwise?
You want control,
a telegenic smile, a jet-ski
—not some St. Bartholomew skinned alive.

I don't begrudge you
your preference for the verifiable
or blame you for your faith
in statistical analyses.

But I liked my scrappy old life,
its grieving voices.
Must everything be buried
in subaqueous crud?

Where are they, the Yorick skull I kept
on top of my field guide to the birds,
the girl I medically examined
behind the furnace when we were eight?

What of the desire
that torched us at seventeen,
that we have survived
and now shun, an illegal minor deity?

Show me the creatures out of Bosch,
the beaked things
that skated through my nightmares,
deepening my love of the light.

With what vengeance
will they all return
—what was once loved or feared,
the ineffable, trashed like a radioactive rod.

I want to drag
the waste containers up,
give the stench
a little time,

then try to free
what you've so confidently
sealed and thrown away
for the sake of self-esteem;

I'll hit the bolted waste containers
with Zuni rockets
in a surgical strike,
an accurate word

opening them up
so that even a child
unaware of the detonation
might see the nimbus and understand.

Party on the Boat

Night lights running on the Hudson,
    the city's reciprocal
sparkling phenomenon
    just off our drunken starboard rail.
You wished you could, like the girdered city,
    throw off all that metal and cement
to lie on the water, brilliantly
    abstracted in a finer element.
I had to hold you back from diving in
    to the breathtaking water lights
beckoning, sequins of gasoline,
    under the George Washington Bridge,
    that pent-up overlord booming all night
       from the pylons and cables of his cage.

Full of Days

Who are you to hope that you could know
the malignancies to be brought down
against you or the powers that contend
above an altogether blameless house,
hating you and ready at a word
to blight the grapes and lay to waste the wall
and send you packing in a place of hail,
simplified, where caltrops have been thrown
along the path? Because the troubles come
at random and unfathomably,
you'll be too blinded by your tears to know
what spike-fisted butcher of a god
has touched the things you love. What good is it
even to think about reprieve, gutted
and unhinged in the trench as you are,
deprived and thrown away?
                                        Consider Job.
What could he have done to fend against
the evils that would screw him to the floor?
In one afternoon, the servants
were all hacked up, the sheep got torched,
and the Chaldeans came down from the hills
gripped by psychotic, spittle-flying rage
and fell upon the camels, and a wind
out of some cursed corner in the wild
smote the gables of his children's house,
obliterating it, with them inside.
Job shaved his head and got down on his knees
and erupted in boils from head to foot.
Then he just sat down in the ashes,
lost in bewilderment and reviled
even by his wife, who counseled him
simply to curse God, lie back, and die.
Never privy to the wagers made,
witnessing only malevolence,

and squatting now on a splintered skid,
Job heard in the tornado touching down
the voice of God commanding him to stand
and look upon the wastes of majesty
and learn, as if by then he might not know,
his place and his provenance. Job then
was reinstated in the grace of God,
his fortunes all abundantly restored,
and Job was, once again, a famous name.
But whether *he* was ever quite the same
or if, in all that later time, the taste
of ashes disappeared, it doesn't say.

Lauterbrunnen

(for Majô)

The mountains also taught us why we speak.
We went into the spaces

below the peaks, to Lauterbrunnen, the waterfalls,
the balconies and beer,
where we drank and spoke about the blue
glaciers, goats, the high-pasture bells,

issues on which nothing seemed to hinge.
We talked about the distances
of the Berner Oberland and how the trains
fed tourists to the fringe.

And it was a sort of victory then,
sitting on the steps of that hotel,
our words like cowbells
tinkering into the desolation.

Le Jardin des Plantes

1. The Watusi

His head, like an Egyptian deity,
governed by two gigantic horns,
is driven by a calm so far beyond the need
to understand his own imprisonment

that it is almost hostile to cognition,
a calm that turns around necessity
—not paralysis or discouragement
from failures or the death of what we love,

but a condition of higher things,
of Cassiopeia, confined in stars,
returning with her two majestic arms
open to the heft of hump and horn.

2. The Cape Vulture

I went there in the cold to look at him,
the retractile wings that erupt like crags
around the head, the bleak hook of the beak,
the vitriolic eye. Thinking of him
as a representative of evil,
I'm guilty of ascribing to this bird
the congenital defect of my race,
a disconsolation of my own.
I need to build a better bridge
going always further out,
that I might touch this bird,
an incarnation of hunger and flight.

3. The Panther

Resting up there in a patch of sun,
remote, he seems to be beyond the cries
from the bright meaningless disks of children
that shift and drift and disappear outside.

A green eye opens when the monkey screams,
and a muscle tightens the jet-black face
that looks away, in a sort of dream,
to three llamas in their fenced-in space.

A memory is dwelling in the deep,
contained quietly with other forces
waiting for articulation, the leap
to ecstasy among the llamas.

4. The Orangutan

Like him, his name here is an oddity.
Mothers mouth it with wonder and fear,
watching him as though he were a monster
in the house for the criminally insane.
Pongo pygmaeus: an anthropoid ape.
But back in the mountains of Borneo
his name means Old Forest Man.
A legend says the gentle being
came from an ancient line of lonely men
who hid in the forests and were silent
not because they could not speak
but because they'd chosen not to.

The Condition

If I could stay awake for centuries,
living on locusts
out where the desert says,
"It is not in *me*,"

or "up unto the watch-towre get,"
where the hail hits,
to "see all things
despoiled of fallacy"

—that would be ideal,
no more the question of career.
But I know none of it
here by the gratings.

A hard time
stuck in the storm station,
trains always late,
snow that dumps down vengefully

like some heavenful
of angels blown to smithereens
—not what I'd been hoping for.
Still, it's not so bad,

the wintering through winter,
companion of owls.
Even the Union Terminal Cold Storage Building #3
stands out there vaguely in the snow,

doubting itself,
all structures,
the downhearted machines
regretting their immobility

and that pig-iron rule: no ideas
but in things. Given a chance,
the gantry cranes would lust
after some voluptuous

and wholly unindustrial idea,
the merest of Platonic wisps
upon which everything would turn,
whimsical spindle of necessity.

All these things would come to naught
were they deprived of refuge
in the condominiums of thought,
where they might rest a little while

from the ravagings. For them, too,
I stay up late, in the lode,
to get the words
for every boreal admonishment.

The Shearwater

Closing on the littoral, this bird
coming down from Arctic seas
but still beyond the telescopic world
confounds the Chrysler falcons we *can* see
mortified in chrome. There's nothing here
that cannot be perpetually deduced
from those more elemental spheres,
where the far flyer, loosed
in empty zones, disdaining the fjord,
runs out the night in gales
somewhere off the coast of that Labrador
deep inside the ear—it never fails
to clip and glide, the name itself
in winter's weather, places hard to tell.

Snowed In, Sparrowbush, New York

(for Pat McWilliams)

Now is not the time for ornament.
Out here at the edge,
a white birch bends down,
and a chickadee puts up six
impenitent notes against the cold.

The woods, all white and silent,
will not suffer anything
beneath their own severity.
How they would scowl
if some inessential leaf
hindered the physics of the wind.

The old limestone wall,
druidical and undeceived,
hobbles toward a northern corner of the property
where deer sometimes materialize
like words one never hoped to find.

And what about the birds?
Even the chickadee would sneer
if the blue-headed vireo,
a summer bird, came north
and froze to death predictably.
The black-capped picker in the ice
has earned the right to know
the extraneous cannot be beautiful.

The starlings, those chore boys,
know that this is not a time for flight
but for perching and reclusion.
In the falling snow
they just sit in the apple tree

retreating into themselves,
lowly, triangular, obdurate.
How paltry, in their black BB eyes,
my shovel up against the door.

Three Landscapes

1. Before Dawn, Orange County, New York

Nothing but to go
and just be gone,
a good road
out of Wawayanda
where the iron works are.

At least another hour left of night.
It's gravel time,
ratchet wheel, good-bye.
No one up ahead
or back behind,
the cold air only,
a low meadow
where the mist makes it,
and whatever star that is
out above a steeple to the west.
Beyond the pick-up-truck-and-trade-in towns
the road's laid down
like track
through the ruin of things.

A blinking light
ten miles out of Middletown
does a job for no one
in the fourth watch of the night.
Nothing is much given
to being known.
A few words come
that you can hammer and
lay in deep
to salvage what goes without saying.

2. Rock Concert, the Meadowlands, New Jersey

Tailgate city, Hibachis everywhere,
the smell of cooked meat rising from Lot 7
like hecatombs to the radio tower
and its one, undiscriminating light.
Behind us, white and rectilinear,
the arena rises against a sky
as blue as copper acetate
west of the New Jersey Turnpike.

We live for a while in the amplified sound,
the bass reconstituting our bones,
all the mewling passions
transubstantiated into thunder.
Even the rock deity,
Dionysian gift to the world,
works to hold his own
against the unpent force of our applause.

Back in Union City we go to bed
smelling of diesel fuel
and dream about the fans in limbo,
hoarse, beery, blinded
in a way they've come to know,
each one a shade
that held a Telecaster once
in some long-dead garage band.

3. Hoboken, New Jersey

The cormorant, the bilious gull,
the scoured Hudson bright this morning
in big October wind,
and the pigeons, down and out,
missing their appointments
to loiter on the dock with me.

How deluded to believe
that things *don't* come to grief
when they fall in upon themselves,
as they do in a confraternity of rust
from here to Philadelphia.
It is enough, perhaps, to recognize
our own fatigue
in what utility has left behind.

Lacrimae Rerum

1. Wind and Dust

One day, perhaps, you'll be there, coming out
along the northbound tracks
by pitted concrete walls, the metal arches
of an overpass, a flight of rusty stairs
secured by nothing really, a few spikes
weakened from exposure.
By then your face may have taken on
the look of St. Jerome,
who carried bags of sand along the edge
of the Red Sea, hoping thus
to interrupt the mind's recursion.
How far can you go, what can you hear
in the howl set up among
these fourteen echoing stanchions?

2. Challenger

Sixty-one skies were clear,
the winds light, as usual,
the tracking cameras on but standing by.

Technicians worked a stubborn bolt.

We're down, of course, but it isn't as if
we've lost all time.

The drill's battery failed
so another drill was sent
but the titanium chewed up the drill bit
and a hacksaw was delivered
to cut through the ice,
and when the hacksaw cut away the bolt
the hatch handle came down.

        *   *   *

Five hundred thousand gallons
of flammable control
feeding the fire geyser,
the gleaming thing aloft,
risen off the pad,
but everyone said afterwards
it was too terrible to believe,
the way it flew apart
and spun away and split,
and they could only watch the thing
break up in a boiling ball.

It's become forgotten,
how it really is.

The networks got involved
in the blown telemetry
deep in the downrange,
developing footage

into a sequence to spin out
in that final ten-second engine blast
filmed for distribution.

*   *   *

Though it was something
that was our mind,
and we were thunderstruck,
it did not change
the state of things,
the television spectacle,
the millions coming out to see
the rupture of knowing
where space starts,
at seventy-five miles up.

*   *   *

There had been the faulty part,
the throttling down,
the spewing of burning pieces,
and someone said they had been
professionals in the fireball.
No personal effects were found,
just bits of debris:
some bulkhead-type material,
aluminum with insulation
and fifteen-foot aluminum sections,
and two dangerous cone-shaped objects,
and a large piece with wiring
for a large piece with gauges,
and several small cylinder-type tanks and things,
and some heat-repelling tiles,
and some five-foot things with wires
lifted out of the waves.

3. Voyager 2, An Elegy

Stowed aboard the Pioneer *and* Voyager *space probes are terrestrial artifacts that include etchings of a naked man and woman and samples of recorded music.* Voyager 2 *carries the* Cavatina *from Beethoven's* String Quartet Number 13. *By now these probes have left the solar system.*

A thankless task, to talk about the stars.
Cold and uncharitable, worse than Mars,
      they are forever put upon, and much
            they've had to bear, from all the rhapsodies
of helmsmen on December nights to the stark
      etchings and the music of *this* sphere launched
            toward the ancient, unimpinging ones.
Tonight, though, no one cares about the stars.

Circumspect like us, they come across
as something other, something less
      than what we'd hoped they'd be,
            not so much angelic as thermonuclear,
a blue giant here, there a dwarf, leaving space
      for the reeling of astronomy's
            celestial math prodigiously applied
to luminosity and dust.

We've sent our intricate, unmanned wizards out
(each perfectly selfless, a master scout)
      to work remotely and to sweep beyond
            the beltway of the asteroids, at last
to send us bits of data back about
      the altogether ice-encased,
            deep-blue methane face of Neptune,
a portrait done in signals dying out.

After that, it's deep-space listening,
for years the task of tracking
            where they go, these things, and what they've found to say
                        to Pluto softly as they pass
and cross the heliopause, waving
            almost, as one might wave who goes away
                        forever, but with a promise still
to write a brief letter every evening.

A face of steel and light titanium
readjusts its eye as the sun's
            diminished winds die into the galactic wind
                        of a hundred billion stars,
the heavens, then, only a tedium
            of wavering densities adrift within
                        themselves, and nothing anyone can do
the day there is no more plutonium.

Once this, the generator's fuel, is gone,
then all volition will be gone,
            the ghost given up, the craft
                        though fallen silent still moving out
with Ludwig's *Cavatina*, borne
            toward that place the charts
                        call Ursa Minor, forty thousand years away
in the hospice of light and time.

4. Techne's Clearinghouse

(George Washington Bridge, New York City)

Bridge out there in the big cold,
a bare location,
my storm-colored dominator

of ten million rivets
illumined in a nighttime
to which large things belong,

I want not just to speak to you,
but for you somehow to understand,
that I might make my way

a little less harrowingly
in the dispensation of things.
I've seen you on the long approach,

clean as a differential equation
strung between the Cloisters and the cliffs,
and I've fallen more than half in love

with planes of shifting light,
the diamonds in the traffic's lit-up veins,
and the voice of your megalomania:

like the sound of trains,
a deep angelus going out
to all the equipment we've devised,

the F-16, the dirty winch,
the cyclohexane refinery,
and your fair sister of the other side,

thrown and fury-fused,
who knows too well this litany.
I've been too long among these things,

too quiet, objectified like them,
using *thing* to indicate
whatever does its time

in Techne's clearinghouse,
only now to find myself
inside among machinery

and fouled with distribution.
How far have we let it go,
the estrangement,

a bad marriage to utility
blinding us to higher purpose?
It's been too long,

this living, mute and paralyzed,
at the foot of buildings
as we've conceived them till now,

the windy interchangeables.
My talking to you helps allay
the fear, always with me,

that you, the sad king of induration,
may be too far gone to understand.
Lording your geometry and lights,

you're everything I've always dreamed
the mineral kingdom could become.
What am I left with

when I need to speak of you,
an angle-iron deity
of arch, thrust, interval,

too big now for the name of *thing*,
an evacuated word. Yet if any
cleated spectacle can justify

that old capacious name, it's you,
Mammon's Harp, a system
for celebrating steel

while the bells ring out in pandemonium.
There is no end
to the trouble of things,

their gravity and fatigue.
Maybe I can help you in a way,
inured as I am, all my kind,

to wandering about, trying to make do
in a blizzard of phenomena.
Susceptible as I am

to every ghost of every chance,
I know that more inheres
than the trigonometric logic

you're so terribly welded to,
my real and glittering interlocutor.
Leaving, as I must,

the fixations of the engineer,
and risking reprisal
to listen in on what goes on

way up there in the cables
and towers in the wind,
I put these words to you.

Paterfamilias

(John C. W. Foy, 1919-1997)

I try to think of what I'd say
were you to come back tonight,
sublunary though not
entirely terrestrial,
wanting maybe to come home
and talk about the howitzers,
the shelling, and the hail.

I know that if I tried
to reach for you, to hold you in my arms,
I'd fail the way Aeneas did
in that pathetic underworld,
where three times he tried
to apprehend what he had loved,
and the has-beens laughed by Cocytus.

Clear-headed now, with eyes rinsed out
by rain, no more the fool,
I wouldn't ask you why you'd come
or how it was contrived, though I
would tell you all about
Catherine and Christopher
—Christopher you never knew.

Ice-Chopping Tool

How unbecoming to be envious
of the rake's chatter, the sprinkler's voice,
the broom's moderate discourse with the dust
—all these languages with no more choice
than I, my winter tongue more capable
of celebrating *this* environment,
the gritty ice impenetrable
to all except an edge violent
and hard enough to meet its object face
to face and come away bright, unbent,
more punishing than punished by the ice,
a season to test out my temperament.

NOTES

Eucalyptus Trees (pages 5-7)

The word *saudade*, in line 25, used all the time by Brazilians, denotes homesickness, wistful longing, regret, or nostalgia.

Ouro Prêto (pages 11-13)

Ouro Prêto, a seventeenth-century town in the state of Minas Gerais, is known for its Baroque architecture, religious art, and School of Mines. Its economy is based on mining and metallurgy. Antonio Dias is the name of a church; *favela* is Portuguese for slum; Cachoeira das Andorinhas is the name of a waterfall (Waterfall of the Swallows); *candeia* is a kind of wood typically burned in fireplaces.

Ismene (page 16)

Ismene and Antigone were the daughters of Oedipus. Nowhere in Greek literature is there an account of Ismene's death.

Rue des Martyrs (pages 29-39)

Rue des Martyrs is a street in the ninth *arrondissement* of Paris.

Lauterbrunnen (page 51)

A response to Rosanna Warren's poem "Alps," which begins: "The mountains taught us speechlessness."

Le Jardin des Plantes (pages 52-53)

These poems obliquely acknowledge those that Rilke wrote about animals in Le Jardin des Plantes, a botanical garden and zoo in Paris.

The Condition (pages 54-55)

Line 4: *Job* 28:14: "The depth saith, It is not in me."

Stanza two borrows from Donne's "Second Anniversary," lines 293-295:

> Thou look'st through spectacles; small things seeme great
> Below; But up unto the watch-towre get,
> And see all things despoyl'd of fallacies . . .

Lacrimae Rerum (pages 62-69)

The phrase *lacrimae rerum*, "the tears of things," comes from the *Aeneid*, Book I, line 462:

> *sunt lacrimae rerum et mentem mortalia tangunt.*

John Foy is the managing editor in Global High Yield Research at Bear Stearns in New York. His poetry has appeared in *The New Yorker, Poetry, The New Criterion, Parnassus,* and *Southwest Review,* among other journals, as well as on the Internet. He has taught writing at Harvard Business School, Columbia University, and Barnard College, and his reviews have appeared in *Parnassus* and other publications. He has spent much time in France and Brazil and now lives in New York City with his wife, son, and daughter.